To Victor and Abigail,

Enjoy the Journey with Stinky Chubster and me!!

Scot Lance

A Short ~~Tail~~ Tale of Stinky Chubster

Written by Scot Lance and Margarida Lance

Illustrated by David Flood

Copyright © 2014 Scot Lance and Margarida Lance.

All rights reserved. No part of this book may be used or reproduced by any means, graphic, electronic, or mechanical, including photocopying, recording, taping or by any information storage retrieval system without the written permission of the publisher except in the case of brief quotations embodied in critical articles and reviews.

Archway Publishing books may be ordered through booksellers or by contacting:

Archway Publishing
1663 Liberty Drive
Bloomington, IN 47403
www.archwaypublishing.com
1-(888)-242-5904

Because of the dynamic nature of the Internet, any web addresses or links contained in this book may have changed since publication and may no longer be valid. The views expressed in this work are solely those of the author and do not necessarily reflect the views of the publisher, and the publisher hereby disclaims any responsibility for them.

Any people depicted in stock imagery provided by Thinkstock are models, and such images are being used for illustrative purposes only. Certain stock imagery © Thinkstock.

ISBN: 978-1-4808-1185-0 (sc)
ISBN: 978-1-4808-1186-7 (hc)
ISBN: 978-1-4808-1187-4 (e)

Printed in the United States of America.

Archway Publishing rev. date: 10/24/2014

This book is for all animals,
especially those rescued from
animal shelters,
including our beloved little Angel
Better known as Stinky Chubster!

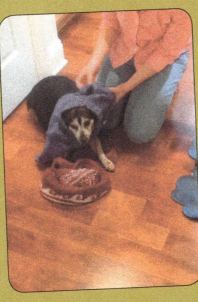

Hello my name is Stinky Chubster.
 I am a minpin. I have a very short tail, but, I have a fun tale to tell you....

Once I was a little puppy, with no family.
Much to my happiness my mommy adopted me from a doggie shelter.
She named me Little Angel.

I am usually a good dog, a very good dog.
Being good is sometimes difficult, because...
I like to bark, but I never bite.

I love to eat way too many treats and I enjoy napping.
These are some of my favorite things to do.

I also love to play Frisbee. In my mind I am the best frisbee catching dog in the world.

For a long time, it was just mommy and me. Life was sweet.
   I was mommy's one and only.
   I am a very, very spoiled dog.
   Mommy loves me and I love Mommy.

Then my mommy met a handsome and kind man whom she fell madly in love with. She married him.

Now I have to share my mommy with my new daddy. We live in a beautiful new house. I have a big back yard to play in.

I sleep in my own big comfy cozy bed.
Life is good.

Daddy has a nickname for me!
He calls me Stinky Chubster!
Why?
I don't like water and I don't like to bathe!

If it rains, I stay indoors. At the seashore I run very fast away from the waves.

If it is cold outside, mommy does not bathe me.
She fears I might catch a cold. Mommy rubs my ears with lavender, so that I don't stink. Mommy doesn't know it, but I don't care for lavender!

I like to be stinky.
   Every chance I get, I roll around in the grass and dirt to be stinky again!

So, what's up with the chubster part?

Once upon a time, I was little and slim, now that I am older I am still little but not so slim.

I don't like canned dog food.

Among my favorite treats are steak, mac and cheese, cupcakes, ice cream and jelly beans!

Did I forget to mention I love steak? Through the years I have put on a few extra pounds.

Since Mommy and I have lived with Daddy he has put on a few pounds too!

Daddy is kind of chunky himself.

So, enough about me and how Daddy started calling me stinky chubster.

Let's go on to one of my favorite tales:

Mommy normally walks me daily in the afternoon.

Our neighborhood is pretty but very busy.

There are lots of houses and lots of cars on the roads.

If mommy is too busy, Daddy walks me.

I don't mind because Daddy takes me for longer and more fun walks.

I like to stop along the way and sniff what my doggie friends have been up to.

One late afternoon, daddy was dressed up to take mommy out to dinner. Mommy wasn't ready,
   so daddy took me for my daily walk.
   That afternoon, daddy was in a hurry.
   He kept giving me a little tug, so I would hurry along.
   Suddenly he tugged a little to strongly.....
   WHOOSH, I easily slipped out of my collar.

He looked at me, I looked at him.
"Here Stinky Chubster, come to daddy. Lets go home!" he pleaded.
I was not ready to go home.

"Woof, woof"
"WOOF, WOOF"
I took off running at full speed the other way!

I zigged and I zagged across the street and through back yards.

I am a stubborn little dog!
HA! HA! HA! HA!

There was no way daddy was going to catch me.
I jumped over small bushes.

I sneaked under fences. Daddy was trying to catch up but, Daddy is not only chubby, he is also somewhat of a slowpoke.

In the distance, I heard mommy calling for me.

LITTLE ANGEL! LITTLE ANGEL!

I followed her voice I found my way home all on my own!

Daddy came home not knowing the whereabout of stinky chubster.
   Daddy was all sweaty and stinky himself. He saw me curled up under my blankey, comfy and cozy in my bed.

I looked at him and I thought!
HA!HA!HA!HA!

Who is the stinky chubster now?

As you see, I get into lots of mischief, this is just one of the many fun tales I have to tell you..........

CPSIA information can be obtained
at www.ICGtesting.com
Printed in the USA
BVHW022004071221
623448BV00007B/111